DOILY MAGIC™

Sweet & Simple Patchwork

Sharon Rexroad

THROUGH THE SCREEN DOOR
PO Box 505 - DM2
Columbia, MO 65205-0505
Orders (USA): 1-800-889-6213
Phone: 573-256-7078
Website: www.sharonrexroad.com

IN Memory

For Punkin, the cat.

A faithful friend who thought fabric scraps were toys!

Credits

Photography	*Patti Geist, Geist Photography, Kearney, NE*
Printing	*Printed in USA at Morris Press, Kearney, NE*
Text/Illustrations	*Sharon Rexroad*
Proofreading	*Doris McMullen, Linda Rash, Jeanne Thorn*
Quilt Designer	*Sharon Rexroad*
Quiltmakers	*MaryAnn Decker, Linda Rash (embellishments), Sharon Rexroad*

Product Sources

Doily sets for the projects may be available from **THROUGH THE SCREEN DOOR**. Contact us at address on previous page for further information.

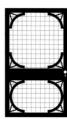

Doily Magic™: Sweet & Simple Patchwork ©
© 1997, Sharon Rexroad-Ericson
Revised 2nd Edition
© 2000, Sharon Rexroad
Through the Screen Door, PO Box 505, Columbia, MO 65205-0505
ISBN: 1-893898-04-0

Printed in the United States of America
04 03 02 01   5 4 3 2

TABLE OF CONTENTS

Chapter	Contents	Page
I	A New Look at Lace	5
II	In Love with Lace	12
III	I ♥ My Secret Sister	16
	Gallery of Doily Magic Quilts	**21**
IV	Tea Cozy	29
V	Symphony of Lace	32
VI	Drunkard's Doilies	36
VII	Do - Si - Doilies	40
VIII	Lace & Marmalade	44
	Sources of Specialty Items	48

Chapter 1
THE MAGIC OF DOILIES

Isn't It Romantic?

SuccesSecret
Be on the lookout for notes in this column. These special hints will help make your finished project spectacular!

SuccesSecret
Don't forgot the final step -- Letting your friends "ooh!" and "ah!" over you and your quilt!

A New Look at Lace

You're invited to join me in a journey through the magical world of doily patchwork™. This world is inhabited by a wide variety of laces -- cluny hearts, battenburg, crocheted irish roses and pineapples, tatted, and fabric centered doilies. But the doilies don't stand alone -- each is paired with a wonderful fabric that brings another dimension to the lace. The end result may be charming, light-hearted, dramatic, sophisticated, elegant, or rustic -- but it's always romantic!

One of the best things about Doily Magic™ quilts is that they have the visual complexity of heavily pieced or appliqued quilts, but with only a quarter of the work! Doily patchwork is amazingly simple to make -- all it takes is a glue stick, a square of fabric and a doily. The basic process consists of these steps:

- Visually dividing a square of fabric into halves or quarters
- Positioning a doily over the square of fabric
- Gluing the doily to the fabric with a light touch
- Cutting the doilied-square into sections
- Rearranging the sections into a pleasing arrangement
- Piecing the sections together just like regular patchwork
- Quilting through doily edges to hold them down permanently

Doilies are normally referred to by *size* (examples: 4", 10", 18"), *style* (examples: tatted, battenburg, pineapple), and *shape* (examples: round, square, heart). Doily Magic quilts can be made from any size or design of doilies, but normally use only round doilies. In addition -- and this is the critical factor in making successful Doily Magic quilts -- we must now look at doilies and count the *number of scallops*. It is this factor that determines for which kind of patchwork design a specific doily can be used.

At its most extreme, a doily may be cut into as many patchwork segments as there are scallops -- an eight scallop doily into eight segments, a fourteen scallop doily into fourteen segments, and so on. Your larger doilies with lots of scallops could actually be transformed into Mariner's Compass quilts.

SuccesSecret
Battenburg doilies may have more than one scallop type built into their design pattern. Count repeats of major motifs to determine number of scallops.

For the purposes of this book, however, we are restricting ourselves to dividing doilies into two or four patchwork segments. Doilies with either an odd or even number of scallops can be effectively halved. Only doilies with an even number of scallops *and* with the additional restriction that the number of scallops can be easily divisible by four can be effectively quartered. If you don't follow these guidelines, your finished doily patchwork will appear unbalanced. The flowchart which follows helps you decide if a particular doily works for a specific project:

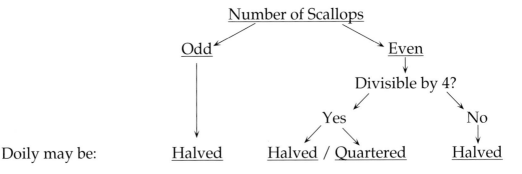

Doily : Square Size Ratio

Once a doily has been selected for a certain design, the size of the square to place it on must be determined using the following three factors:

- The smaller the doily, the smaller the margin needed around doily
- Doilies are not <u>exact</u> sizes; they tend to run smaller than stated size
- Always allow for 1/4" seam allowances on cut blocks

Small (4") doilies can be on squares cut as close as 1 1/4" or as much as 2" bigger than the doily. Medium size doilies (6" - 8") should have margins of 1 1/2" to 3". Larger doilies (10" and up) can handle margins of 2" to 4".

The chart on the following page shows common Doily Magic measurements. There are two basic ways to use it:

1) If your block or quilt doesn't have to be a specific size, I recommend starting out with an easy to cut fabric size from the second column-- something that ends with no fractions or at most, 1/4" or 1/2" (*examples*: 10", 9 1/4", 12 1/2"). The first column tells you what size doily to buy and the last three columns tell you how big your blocks will end up, depending on how you cut your square. This method was used for most quilts in this book.

2) Sometimes, though, a Doily Magic block needs to be a certain size, either because of how big or small the quilt has to end up, or because the Doily Magic block is being combined with other blocks and all measurements must work together. In this case, find the desired finished measurement in one of the last three columns, and work backwards to column two to find out how big to cut your fabric square and column one to find the appropriate size of doily. *Lace and Marmalade*, page 28, was created using this type of scenario.

DOILY MAGIC SIZE CHART

Doily Size	Size of Fabric Square	Quartered Square Corners	Finished Size of Square Using	
			Half Square Triangles	Quarter Square Triangles
4"	5"	2"	4 1/8"	3 3/4"
	5 1/8"	2 1/16"	4 1/4"	3 7/8"
	5 1/4"	2 1/8"	4 3/8"	4"
	5 3/8"	2 3/16"	4 1/2"	4 1/8"
	5 1/2"	2 1/4"	4 5/8"	4 1/4"
	5 5/8"	2 5/16"	4 3/4"	4 3/8"
	5 3/4"	2 3/8"	4 7/8"	4 1/2"
	5 7/8"	2 7/16"	5"	4 5/8"
	6"	2 1/2"	5 1/8"	4 3/4"
6"	7 1/4"	3 1/8"	5 3/8"	5"
	7 3/8"	3 3/16"	5 1/2"	5 1/8"
	7 1/2"	3 1/4"	5 5/8"	5 1/4"
	7 5/8"	3 5/16"	5 3/4"	5 3/8"
	7 3/4"	3 3/8"	5 7/8"	5 1/2"
	7 7/8"	3 7/16"	6"	5 5/8"
	8"	3 1/2"	6 1/8"	5 3/4"
	8 1/8"	3 9/16"	6 1/4"	5 7/8"
	8 1/4"	3 5/8"	6 3/8"	6"
8"	9 1/2"	4 1/4"	8 5/8"	8 1/4"
	9 5/8"	4 5/16"	8 3/4"	8 3/8"
	9 3/4"	4 3/8"	8 7/8"	8 1/2"
	9 7/8"	4 7/16"	8"	8 5/8"
	10"	4 1/2"	9 1/8"	8 3/4"
	10 1/8"	4 9/16"	9 1/4"	8 7/8"
	10 1/4"	4 5/8"	9 3/8"	9"
	10 3/8"	4 11/16"	9 1/2"	9 1/8"
	10 1/2"	4 3/4"	9 5/8"	9 1/4"
10"	11 1/2"	5 1/4"	10 5/8"	10 1/4"
	11 5/8"	5 5/16"	10 3/4"	10 3/8"
	11 3/4"	5 3/8"	10 7/8"	10 1/2"
	11 7/8"	5 7/16"	11"	10 5/8"
	12"	5 1/2"	11 1/8"	10 3/4"
	12 1/8"	5 9/16"	11 1/4"	10 7/8"
	12 1/4"	5 5/8"	11 3/8"	11"
	12 3/8"	5 11/16"	11 1/2"	11 1/8"
	12 1/2"	5 3/4"	11 5/8"	11 1/4"

Selecting Base Fabrics

Doilies add a softness or intensity of design depending upon the patterns in the fabrics with which they are combined. If there is high contrast between doily and fabric, the result is dramatic; if low contrast, the effect is subdued.

One issue to consider is doily color. Stark white doilies work well with fully saturated, strong colors. Ecru doilies look best on more muted or toned down colors. This is not to say ecru doilies are paired with weak-looking fabrics; in fact, the richer the fabric color, the richer the final quilt looks.

SuccesSecret
See page 28 for white doilies on saturated colors; pages 24-25 for ecru doilies on muted, yet rich, fabrics; page 25 for a variety of tone-on-tone fabrics; page 26 for plaid; page 24 for subtlety; and page 27 for an example of medium-light fabric.

Another consideration is fabric pattern and contrast of colors within the fabric itself. Tone-on-tone base fabrics with low to medium contrast don't compete with the doily placed on them. Don't, however, fall into the trap of using only tiny prints. In fact, keep the scale of the fabric pattern in line with the size of the doily: small doilies -> small prints; large doilies -> large prints.

Just because doilies are romantic, don't think you can't use plaids. In fact, plaids, checks, stripes and other geometric patterns form a wonderful juxtaposition to the laciness of doilies. Keep the contrast of colors within the geometric fabric medium to low -- if high contrast, it may overwhelm doily.

Finally, unless you are looking for an extremely subtle and serene look, make sure the base fabric has enough color for the doily to easily show up on it. In general, your palest base fabric should be medium-light in tone.

Fabric Preparation

Prewash all fabrics, especially dark toned blues, reds and blacks, either by hand or in your machine's delicate cycle. Use a gentle soap designed for quilts. If you're one of those folks who just toss your quilts in with your regular laundry soap -- and you know who you are -- prewash using a touch of that detergent.

SuccesSecret
Time spent up front preparing fabric is time well spent -- after your quilt is finished is not the time to discover your red fabric has turned your doilies pink!

Check each dark fabric separately. If needed, wash several times. Although I haven't seen actual scientific proof, soaking fabric in a vinegar/non-iodized salt bath may help. Use 1/2 cup vinegar and 1/2 cup salt per gallon of water - they're inexpensive compared to your anguish if your finished quilt is ruined.

If you're concerned about color run after three washings, test your fabric by sewing a scap of white fabric to it and then wash again. If color gets on the white fabric, discard the culprit. If excess dye just floats in the water but doesn't settle on the white fabric, go ahead and use it.

SuccesSecret
Starched fabric easily supports the added weight of doilies.

If I could give just one hint for successful machine piecing, it would be to STARCH YOUR FABRIC. Not only does your machine love a stiff fabric, but bias seams are less likely to stretch out of shape. If you quilt by hand, use spray sizing. If quilting by machine, use professional strength spray starch. The best method for using the starch is to prewash your fabric, dry it on low until barely damp to the touch, spray it with starch or sizing, then iron.

Doily Preparation

SuccesSecret
June Tailor™ Cut-and-Press or Blocking Boards work great.

Most doilies are made of 100% cotton and should therefore be prewashed. This is especially critical for pre-dyed doilies, such as those used for Drunkard's Doilies (shown page 26). Although colors in quality brands won't run, better safe than sorry! First, dip doily in warm water. Then lay doily on thick terry cloth towel and place second towel (or excess from original towel) over doily. Roll towel(s) up and wring out excess moisture. Dry until just barely damp in dryer.

Lay doily flat on blocking board and pin in position so all sides are evenly distributed around the doily center and scallops lie flat. Let dry completely.

Positioning & Gluing Doilies

The first step in making an actual Doily Magic block is to mark lines on the right side of fabric square(s). These lines divide the block into halves or quarters. They may run through block center either vertically and horizontally, or diagonally.

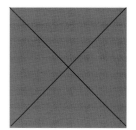

SuccesSecret
Doilies with an odd number of scallops are treated differently, as described on page 34.

The doily may then be positioned over the line(s). Lay fabric square right side up on a surface into which you can put pins. Put pin through center of both doily and square and then into padded surface. Rotate doily until 'valleys' between the scallops are directly over crease lines in square.

Lift doily off fabric and use a purple disappearing glue stick to lightly glue around doily edges and over part of doily that will go over lines on fabric square. If you plan to quilt motifs inside the doily in addition to the edges, glue over these as well.

SuccesSecret
Both Avery and UHU brand glue sticks work well.

Use a *very light touch* and a dabbing motion -- you want your needle to be able to get through the glue later on! The small .28 ounce glue stick is best; the larger size gets gloppy.

SuccesSecret
Buy 3 or 4 glue sticks; keep them in coldest part of refrigerator or in freezer. Rotate use when one gets too sticky.

Place doily back over fabric square, matching centers and keeping 'valleys' over lines. Lightly press from the wrong side with iron.

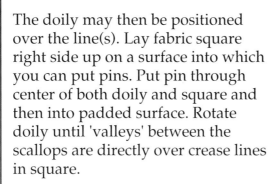

Glue on just edges & over lines

Glue on edges, over lines & major motifs

Cut & Sew; Sew & Cut

The cut & sew or sew & cut sequence varies depending on final block style. If the patchwork involves squares, you will most likely cut fabric and doily apart on lines, then sew the units together after cutting.

SuccesSecret
Proper cutting and sewing sequence is in each project's instructions.

If the patchwork involves triangles, you most likely will lay another fabric square right sides together over the doilied fabric, sew the two together and then cut apart into separate units.

When you sew, use a *short stitch length* (1.5-2 on European manufactured sewing machines; 15-18 stitches per inch on American machines) and an 80/12 sewing machine needle.

Regardless of whether cutting or sewing comes first, press seams away from doilies except when doilies end up in the same seam (as with Drunkard's Doilies, p. 36) or when doily tips meet at a four-part block's center (as with Do-Si-Doilies, p. 40). In these instances, press seams open with raw doily edge and fabric both pressed back over the 'doilied' fabric.

Quilting Options

If the quilt is to be hand quilted, slip stitch doily edges to fabric after all cross seams have been sewn. Use thread to match doily. Layer back, batting and quilt top. Echo quilt in fabric around doily edges and fabric seams.

SuccesSecret
Buy extra needles -- they break!

If machine quilting, layer back, batting and quilt top; doilies are just glued to fabric and caught in seams at this point. Free-motion quilt through doilies and layers using a 90/14 specialty quilting needle or a 100/16 jeans needle.

Lace Edged Quilts

Inserting lace into the edge of a quilt is a pretty alternative to traditional binding methods and complements the doilies used in the quilts. The basic method for inserting lace is as follows:

SuccesSecret
Start adding lace one-third of the way up the right hand side of quilt and run it down towards lower right corner.

Lay lace right sides together over edge of quilt top. Position lace relative to edge so that the 1/4" seam will fall at a "pretty" spot on lace. Straight edge of lace may or may not fall exactly at raw edge of quilt top; it may be over edge or be inside it.

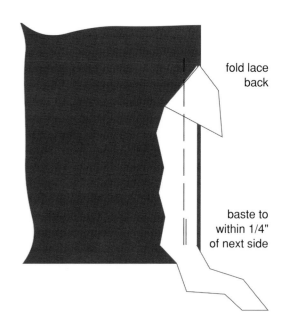

fold lace back

baste to within 1/4" of next side

Diagonally fold end of lace back on itself. Raw end extends past straight edge of lace and hangs into seam allowance.

Machine baste a scant 1/4" from edge. Stop basting 1/4" from next side (first corner); backbaste.

SuccesSecret
For very full and gathered corners (see p. 25), baste for an additional design repeat.

Remove quilt top from under machine needle. Identify which design element on the lace hits right at the corner. Visually move down the free-hanging lace until a mirror image of that element is found. Hand baste between motifs.

Turn quilt top so next side will go under machine needle. Fold hand basted lace back over first side, then forward over second side; match design motifs on either side of fold. Ends of hand basting will be 1/4" in from both edges. If true mirror images were identified, scalloped edges of lace will match.

SuccesSecret
Baste scant 1/4" seam; it won't show later on!

Machine baste backwards to within 1/4" of first side. Baste forward until next corner is reached. Repeat steps until all four corners are turned.

SuccesSecret
If beginning and end of lace doesn't match perfectly, don't panic; there's so much else going on in the quilt, no one should notice.

Lay lace along final (and first) side. Attempt to match motifs or scallops at end of lace with initial diagonally folded beginning of lace. Run extra lace off edge. Machine baste final side, including overlapped laces.

Gather up tightly the hand basting at each corner. Tie off threads to secure.

Cut batt and back same size as quilt top. Layer batt, quilt top with lace (right side *up*), and quilt back (right side *down*). Pin edges of first side together. Manipulate gathers at first corner to be out of way of seam.

SuccesSecret
Begin stitching on first side at about the halfway point; use backstitches. When you get back around to that side, leave a gap for turning quilt right side out; backstitch.

Stitch 1/4" from edge along first side, stopping and backstitching 1/4" from corner. Pull out from under machine needle; manipulate corner gathers to be out of way of second seam (pushed towards first side). Pin second side up to next corner. Stitch and repeat on all sides.

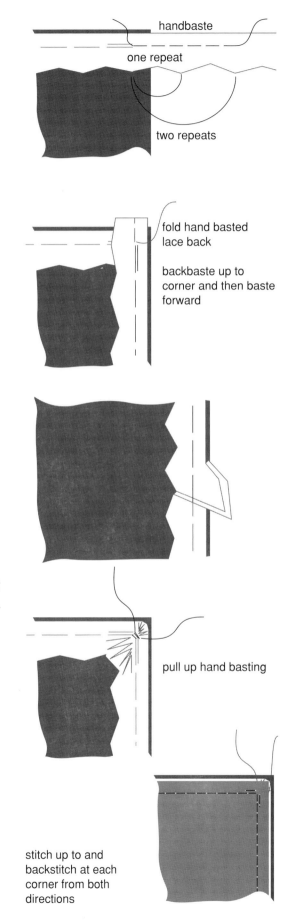

handbaste

one repeat

two repeats

fold hand basted lace back

backbaste up to corner and then baste forward

pull up hand basting

stitch up to and backstitch at each corner from both directions

Chapter 2
IN LOVE WITH LACE

Fabrics and Notions

SuccesSecret
Mix up the scale and style of prints. Heavier doilies can be on bolder patterns.

8" White or White/Ecru Doilies with Eight (8) Scallops	6
1" wide White Crocheted Cotton Lace *for edge of quilt*	6 yds
Focus Floral *for border*	1 1/4 yd
Six (6) Different Pinks/Roses/Peaches	3/8 yd each
White-on-white *for lattice*	1/2 yd
Green w/small flowers *for lattice*	1/8 yd
Backing fabric: 44" x 54"	1 5/8 yd

Batt (pure white won't show through): 44" x 54" crib size
Thread: white for piecing; white for quilting.

Cutting Instructions

SuccesSecret
Prewash and <u>starch</u> fabrics before cutting. This gives fabric enough body to support doilies.

<u>Focus Floral:</u> Cut four *lengthwise* 6 1/2" strips. Set aside for later use.

<u>Each of 6 Pink/Rose/Peach Fabrics:</u> Cut one strip 10" wide; crosscut one 10" square. Cut strip down to 9 3/4"; crosscut and set aside one 9 3/4" square. Cut one 6 1/2" segment and one 5" segment; crosscut each into four 2" wide segments.

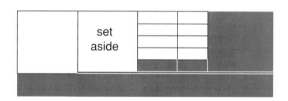

Cut the 9 3/4" square diagonally in half. Cut one of the triangles in half on the 2nd diagonal, forming two right triangles with long edges of 9 3/4" and short edges just over 6 7/8". Cut a 5 1/8" square from other triangle, one corner of which will be nipped off; discard small side triangles. Cut square diagonally in half; discard half with nippedcorner. Remaining triangle will be 7 1/2" on long edge and 5 1/8" on short edges.

12

*I*N *L*OVE WITH *L*ACE

Photograph on page 22

Finished Size:
42 7/8" x 51 2/3" plus lace edging

Blocks including border: 22 total (4 per fabric)
Finished Size: 6" (6 1/2" w/seam allowance)

Side Blocks: 10
Corner Blocks: 4

Mix of 6 Pinks/Roses/Peaches

Focus Floral

White-on-White

Green with Small Flowers

– – White Quilting Thread

Cutting Instructions (continued)

SuccesSecret
If needed, ignore grainlines when centering flowers. Have flowers growing up in 'on point' square.

<u>White-on-White</u>: Cut eight 1 1/2" wide strips; crosscut into forty-eight 6 1/2" segments.

<u>Green with Small Flowers</u>: Cut out thirty-one 1 1/2" squares, centering a small flower in each. If not centering flowers, cut one 1 1/2" strip; crosscut into 1 1/2" squares. Cut a short strip 1 1/2" wide; crosscut into enough extra 1 1/2" squares for thirty-one total.

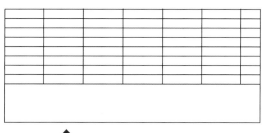

1 1/2" square with flower centered inside 1/4" seam allowances and square set "on point" (on the diagonal)

Make Heart Blocks

SuccesSecret
Mix and match doilies and fabric squares until you get pleasing combinations.

SuccesSecret
Check to make sure block still measures 10" square before cutting apart.

SuccesSecret
Chain stitch all the blocks in sequence, lifting pressure foot as needed to get over doily at start of each seam.

Draw vertical and horizontal center lines on right sides of each 10" pink/rose/peach square. Each line will be 5" from edge.

With fabric right sides up, center doily over each square. Put pin in doily center and through intersection of lines. Rotate doily until lines go through 'valleys'.

Lightly glue doily in place over both lines and along doily edges. Smooth doily in place, but avoid stretching it to the point that the fabric buckles.

Press squares lightly from the wrong side. Cut into quarters using the 5" line on ruler and a rotary cutter/mat.

Stack squares with points of hearts in upper right hand corner. Align matching 2" x 5" rectangle over right edge of square, right sides together. Sew 1/4" seam using a short stitch length; press seam (including doily edge) towards rectangle.

Rotate square so rectangle is at bottom. Match 2" x 6 1/2" rectangle with right edge, right sides together. Sew 1/4" seam; press seam including doily edge towards rectangle. Blocks should be 6 1/2" square.

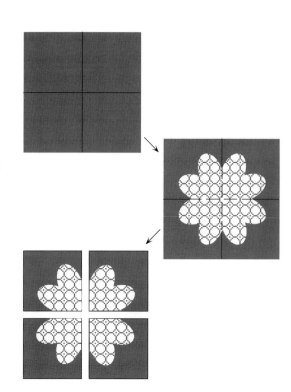

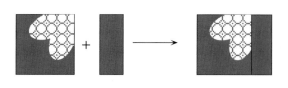

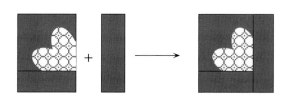

Piece Quilt Top Together

SuccesSecret
Include the border strips in the playing stage -- you'll have a better feel for the overall look.

Lay out heart blocks, side and corner triangles, lattice strips and squares, plus borders for the entire quilt. Spend time playing around with fabric arrangements, referring to photograph on page 22 as needed.

There will be two leftover heart blocks, two leftover side triangles and two leftover corner triangles when you finish arranging the blocks. Discard or make small pillows to match quilt.

Sew blocks and lattice into diagonal rows. Press all seams towards white lattice strips.

SuccesSecret
Butt seams when sewing rows together.

Sew rows together in pairs, then in larger sets. Add corner triangles to complete top. Trim small lattice squares that stick out even with edge of triangles. Press seams to lattice.

Add Borders

SuccesSecret
Measure across quilt's center to determine border lengths -- about 40 1/8" & 31 1/4"

With right sides together, sew border strips to top and bottom edges of quilt; press seams towards border. Sew corner squares to ends of remaining border strips (corners of hearts pointing in); press seams towards border. Butting seams at corners, sew borders to quilt's sides; press seams towards border.

Finish Quilt

SuccesSecret
If you quilt a bit inside edges of doilies, they will ruffle when washed.

Following instructions in Chapter 1, baste lace to edge of quilt top. Layer batt, quilt top (right side up) and backing (right side down). Stitch, leaving 15" opening; turn right side out and close opening. Stretch taut and baste layers together.

Using white thread, quilt all lattice seams "in the ditch". Quilt through edges of doilies. Quilt seams to border. Quilt hearts in border.

Chapter 3
I ♥ MY *S*ECRET *S*ISTER

Fabrics and Notions for Victorian Quilt

SuccesSecret
The richer the colors, the richer the quilt will look!

4" Ecru Doily with Eight (8) Scallops	1
1/4" wide Ecru Cotton Lace with holes *for edge of quilt*	1 1/2 yds
Romantic Print *for corners*	1/4 yd
Burgundy (mottled print) *for blocks*	1/4 yd
Tan tone-on-tone *for lattice*	1/8 yd
Backing fabric: 11" square	1/4 yd in FQ
Batt: 11" square	
Thread: tan for piecing and quilting	
Silk Ribbon, burgundy colored, 3mm	3 yds
1/4"-3/8" Brass Hearts	4
Assorted Glass Beads	

Bodkin for threading ribbon through lace. Beading needle and strong thread for embellishing finished quilt.

Fabrics and Notions for Country Pillow

SuccesSecret
Believe or not, a lace doily on a dark plaid looks great!

4" Ecru Doily with Eight (8) Scallops	1
1 1/2" wide flat Ecru Cotton Lace *for ruffle*	2 1/2 yds
Romantic Print *for corners*	1/4 yd
Burgundy/tan plaid *for blocks, ruffle, pillow back*	1/2 yd
Red-on-tan tiny vine *for lattice*	scraps or 1/8 yd
Backing fabric: *included in plaid above*	
Muslin for pillow form	3/8 yd
Batt: 11" square	
Thread: tan and burgundy for piecing and red for quilting	
Pearl cotton -- Size 8 tan or burgundy	2 1/2 yds
Pillow stuffing (used Fairfield Soft Touch for sample)	

I ♥ MY SECRET SISTER

Photographs on page 23

Finished Size
Victorian:
8 7/8" square
plus 1/4" lace

Finished Size
Country:
8 7/8" square
plus 1 3/4"
ruffle = 12 3/8"

Ruffle for Country Version

Lace for Victorian Version

Blocks: 4
Finished
Size: 2 3/4"
(3 1/4" w/seam
allowance)

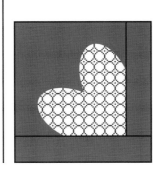

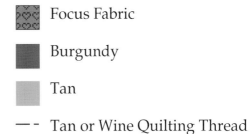

Focus Fabric

Burgundy

Tan

— Tan or Wine Quilting Thread

Cutting Instructions

<u>Romantic fabric</u>: Cut two 6" squares. Cut each square diagonally in half -- if print is directional (that is, if all the hearts go one direction), cut one from upper right to lower left and the other, upper left to lower right.

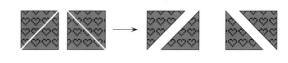

<u>Victorian Burgundy</u>: Cutting parallel to selvage, cut one 5 1/2" strip; crosscut one 5 1/2" square and two 1" strips; crosscut 1" strips into four 2 3/4" segments. Cut one 3 1/4" strip; crosscut into four 1" segments.

Victorian

<u>Country Burgundy/Tan Plaid</u>: Cut three 4" wide bias strips. From corner triangle, cut segments as desribed under Victorian Burgundy. Cut one 9 1/2" strip from longer edge of remaining fabric; crosscut into two 5 1/2" x 9 1/2" rectangles.

Country

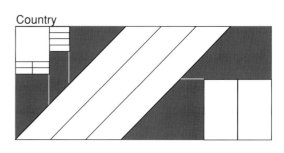

<u>Tan</u>: Cut one 3/4" strip; crosscut into two 3 1/4" segments, three 6 1/4" segments and two 6 3/4" segments.

Make Heart Blocks

Draw vertical and horizontal center lines on right side of burgundy 5 1/2" square. Each line will be 2 3/4" from edge.

With fabric right side up, center doily over square. Put pin in doily center and through intersection of lines. Rotate doily until lines go through 'valleys'.

Lightly glue doily in place over both lines and along doily edges. Smooth doily in place, but avoid stretching it to the point that the fabric buckles.

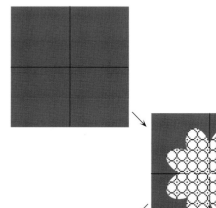

Press square lightly from the wrong side. Cut into quarters using 2 3/4" line on ruler and a rotary cutter/mat. If an irish rose doily, avoid cutting into flowers.

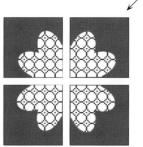

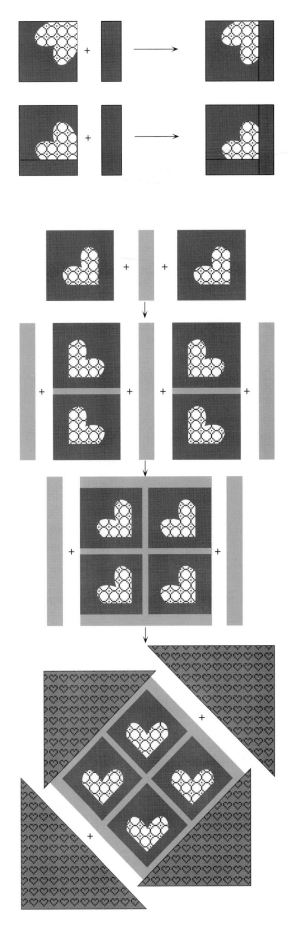

SuccesSecret
Chain sew blocks in sequence, lifting pressure foot as needed to get over doily at start of each seam.

Turn segments so points of hearts are in upper right corner. Align 1" x 2 3/4" rectangle over right edge of square, right sides together. Sew 1/4" seam using a short stitch length; press seam (including doily edge) towards rectangle.

Rotate square so rectangle is at bottom. Lay 1" x 3 1/4" rectangle over right edge, right sides together. Sew 1/4" seam; press seam including doily edge towards rectangle. Blocks should be 3 1/4" square.

Piece Quilt Top Together

SuccesSecret
Sew 'scant' 1/4" seams when adding lattice.

Turn blocks so points of hearts are in lower right corner. Sew 3/4" x 3 1/4" tan strip between two blocks; repeat with remaining two blocks. Press all seams towards blocks.

SuccesSecret
Pressing seams away from lattice makes block come forward and lattice recede in finished quilt.

Turn sections so hearts point to lower left corner. Sew 3/4" x 6 1/4" tan strips between the two sections and to either side. Press all seams towards blocks.

Turn sections so hearts point to lower right corner. Sew 3/4" x 6 3/4" tan strips to both sides. Press all seams towards blocks.

SuccesSecret
Find center of triangle's long side by gently folding in half and finger creasing.

Center long side of Romantic fabric triangle over one side of quilt center, right sides together; tips of triangle will extend 3/4" past both edges. Pin and sew 1/4" seam; avoid overworking bias edge of triangle. Repeat with opposite side. Press seams towards triangle.

SuccesSecret
Have directional prints go same way as hearts.

Center remaining triangles over last two sides. Triangle tips will extend just past end of seam. Pin and sew 1/4" seams; Repeat with opposite side. Press seams towards triangle.

Finishing Victorian Quilt

SuccesSecret
Place 45° line of ruler on lattice/corner triangle seam when trimming square down.

SuccesSecret
Examine the photograph on page 23 for inspiration!

Finishing Country Quilt

SuccesSecret
For full look, make inside pillow 1/4" larger than quilt.

SuccesSecret
Zigzag with burgundy thread so it won't show.

SuccesSecret
Sew to corner, backstitch, stop. Make sure ruffle is stuffed inside; backstitch to start next corner.

Trim quilt so 1/4" extends past points of lattice. Follow instructions in Chapter 1 and baste lace to quilt top so 1/4" will show past quilt edge. Layer batt, quilt top (right side up) and backing (right side down). Stitch, leaving 5" opening; turn right side out and close opening. Stretch taut and baste layers together. Quilt "in the ditch" around each block and at edge of lattice. Quilt doily edges.

Cut 12" lengths of silk ribbon. Use burgundy quilting thread and simultaneously tack center of ribbon and sew brass charm to doily valley. Tie ribbons in bows with 1/2" loops. Manipulate ends to drape over heart, block, lattice and into next block or triangles. Bead ribbon every 1/4".

Bead corner triangles. Run ribbon through holes in edging; tie bow about 2" in from upper right corner.

Baste together quilt top, batt and back. Quilt around squares and at edge of lattice. Trim quilt so 1/4" extends past points of lattice.

Turn long edge of 5 1/2" x 9 1/2" rectangles under 1/4" twice; stitch. Overlap finished edges and baste. Trim to match size of quilt.

Sew 4" bias strips end to end to make continuous ring. Press in half to form 2" wide ring. Machine baste 1 1/2" lace to raw edge. Mark in 8 equal sections. Fabric side up, sew narrow zigzag over pearl cotton 1/4" from edge. Gather up tightly by pulling on pearl cotton; baste onto quilt.

Pin lapped back right sides together over quilt and ruffle; sew 1/4" from edge. Unbaste back, turn and stuff.

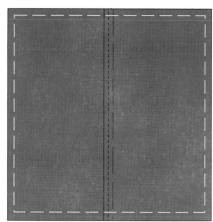

finish back edges, overlap and baste closed; trim

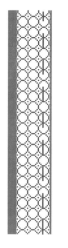

GALLERY OF DOILY MAGIC QUILTS

UNLESS OTHERWISE INDICATED, ALL QUILTS MADE BY SHARON REXROAD

TEA COZY

I made the basic doily tea cozy for my friend, Linda Rash, as a birthday present. She has the most beautiful beige-on-ivory-on-cream living room, so I knew she'd like the subtle contrast of the ecru lace on a delicate white-on-beige print. What I didn't expect was the wonderful bead and button work that she'd add to the tea cozy. Scones, anyone?

Instructions begin on page 29

In Love with Lace

This quilt is just the thing for that special baby girl (or make it for yourself just to wrap up in). It only takes six doilies to make and is easy to do -- just glue, cut and add two strips to each doily quarter and the blocks are done!

Instructions begin on page 12

I ♥ My Secret Sister

Whether you're the secret sister to a lover of Victoriana or a Country devotee, you'll be a hit if you make her this gift. And it only takes one 4" doily!

The little wallhanging is just 9" square and the pillow, including ruffle, only 12 1/2" big. The basic quilt is the same for the two projects -- it's just a matter of fabric choices and embellishments! Speaking of which, my thanks to Linda Rash for her wonderful beadwork on the Victorian wallhanging.

Instructions begin on page 16

Symphony of Laces

This stunning quilt is really quite simple to make. It only takes two fabrics -- a softly patterned focus fabric and a gradated fabric that changes from light to dark between the selvages. The only difficult part was picking out the doilies -- with all the beautiful lace available today, it was hard to restrict myself to just four styles. The end result, though, was definitely worth it.

Instructions begin on page 32

CLOSEUP Look closely and you can see how quilting gives this quilt extra dimension. Not only are the edges of the doilies held in place by the quilting, but so are different design elements within the doilies. Using the second block on the top row as an example, the hearts are quilted at their edges, and the half circle near the center is also quilted down. Note as well the "shadow" quilting in the other half of the blocks -- they are quilted as if there were a doily there. On the back of the quilt, you can't even tell which half has the real doily and which does not.

For your reference, the machine quilting was done using Mettler silk-finish cotton thread and the batting is Hobbs Heirloom Organic Cotton with scrim. The fabric was prewashed and the batt was not; once finished, the whole quilt was washed in lukecool water, partially dried by machine on low heat, then laid flat for final drying. I'm pleased with the end result -- although subtle, the quilting definitely enhances this quilt.

DRUNKARD'S DOILIES

This romantic version of the classic Drunkard's Path quilt uses pre-dyed doilies with fabric centers and battenburg edges. The key to this quilt's success is mixing up the designs in your fabrics, as shown in the closeup.

Instructions begin on page 36

DO-SI-DOILIES

When I was a girl, I used to watch my parents square dance -- and oh, what fun to see lace peeking out from under swirling skirts! This quilt brings back those memories: the block's sides become the four sets of partners, the pinwheels created by the secondary design twirl, and of course, the lace . . .

Instructions begin on page 40

LACE AND MARMALADE

The perfect quilt for a college-bound young woman and, in fact, made by one, MaryAnn Decker. White doilies hold their own against the vibrant colors.

Instructions begin on page 44

Chapter 4
Tea Cozy

Fabrics and Notions

SuccesSecret
Teflon coated fabric is available from Nancy's Notions 1-800-833-0690, or cut up an ironing board cover from discount store!

8" - 14" Matching Ecru Doilies	2
Size dependent on size of tea pot	
Usually, the more scallops, the prettier the tea cozy	
1/4" wide Ecru cotton lace	3/4 to 1 yd
White-on-Cream large scale	3/8 to 1/2 yd
Teflon coated fabric *for lining*	3/8 to 1/2 yd

Batt: Cotton, enough for 4 layers (craft size batt)
Thread: neutral for piecing; ecru for quilting
Assorted clear and cream buttons and beads

Tea Cozy

Photograph on page 21

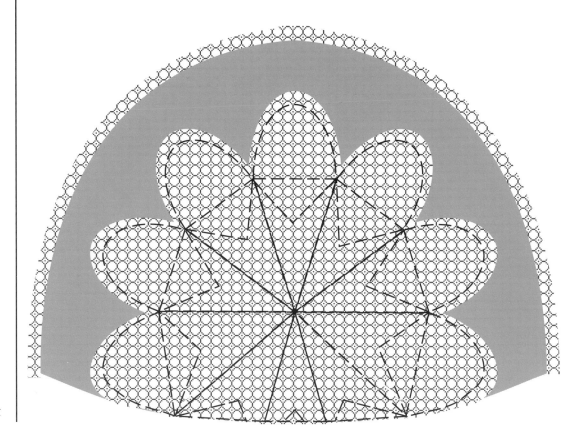

Finished Size:
Varies by teapot

Measure Teapot

Using a cloth tape measure, measure from edge of handle, around fat part of teapot and to tip of spout; round to closest 1" measurement. If tip of spout and handle are "high" relative to height of teapot, subtract 1"; it spout and handle are "normal" relative to height of teapot, do nothing to measurement. Divide measurement in half to get radius of tea cozy.

Measure from fat part of pot straight down to tabletop. Note measurement.

SuccesSecret

Illustrated teapot (modeled after standard Mrs. Tea™ 6-cup pot) measures about 12"; since handle and spout tip are "normal", do nothing to measurement. Tea cozy radius is 12" divided by 2 = 6". 'Fat'-to-table measurement is 2 1/4"

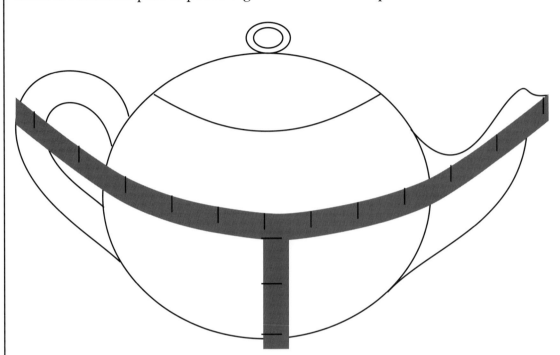

Make Pattern

Take one standard newspaper page, fold in half and then in quarters. Turn so tall fold is to your right.

Measure up from raw edge 'fat'-to-table measurement; draw line parallel to edge. With pivot point being intersection of fold and 'fat'-to-table line, draw quarter circle using tea cozy radius. Draw line straight down to raw edge from end of quarter circle. Measure up 1" from raw edge; mark spot. Draw gradual curve from spot to bottom of fold.

SuccesSecret

Gradual curve at bottom of tea cozy allows it to sit flat to table all way around teapot.

Cut out on lines. Unfold and you will have two elongated half circles. Tape together all along top curved edges. Test fit over teapot; make adjustments as necessary.

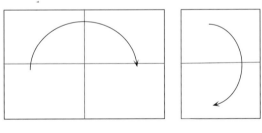

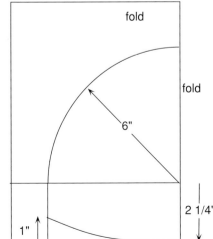

Positioning Doily

Fold fabric with selvages together. Cut two layers 1/2" larger than pattern all the way around. Fold each in half; gently press center line.

SuccesSecret
Doilies should be 1" - 2" smaller than tea cozy measurement. A 12" tea cozy means a 10" doily.

With fabric right sides up, center doily over cozy side. Put pin in doily center and through vertical fold about 'fat'-to-table measurement above lower edge. Rotate doily until it looks balanced. Raise or lower doily along pressed line until 'valleys' line up with lower edge of cozy. *Lightly* glue doily in place along doily edges, under major design motifs and along bottom edge of cozy. Cut excess doily off bottom. Repeat with second cozy side.

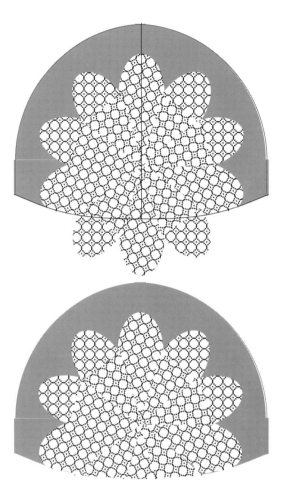

Layer Sides

SuccesSecret
Two layers of batt keep tea warm!

Lay cozy front over tefloned lining; cut two units. Cut four batting layers just bigger than cozy front. Stack two layers of batting, one cozy front (right side up), and lining (tefloned side down); align edges of lining and cozy front. Sew 1/4" from bottom edge. Trim excess batt out of seam, clip as needed and turn inside out: cozy front on top, tefloned lining on back and batting inside. Baste edges.

Baste cozy fronts together (right sides together); turn inside out and verify fit. Take apart.

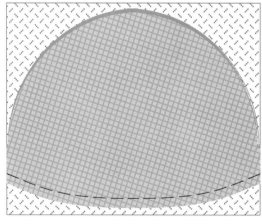

Finish Cozy

SuccesSecret
Trim excess batting out of seam before finishing edges. Zig-zag or serge over seam or french bind.

Machine quilt each cozy side individually through front, batt and back. Quilt around doily edges and through major motifs. Add beads and buttons as desired.

Baste lace to edge of one cozy side, lace facing in. Layer quilted sides right sides together; sew 1/4" seam, backstitching at both ends. Finish raw edges and turn inside out.

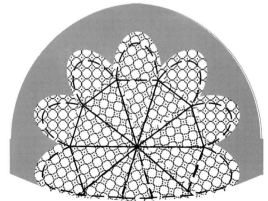

Chapter 5
SYMPHONY OF LACES

Fabrics and Notions

SuccesSecret
Buy both airy and densely crocheted doilies.

SuccesSecret
* Alternately, buy 3/8 yd of light & deep and 1/2 yd of medium & dark.

6" Ecru Doilies (# of scallops irrelevant)	
Style #1 (for light fabric)	4
Style #2 (for medium fabric)	8
Style #3 (for dark fabric)	8
Style #4 (for deep fabric)	4
1" wide Ecru Crocheted Cotton Lace	6 yds
Gradated* Fabric (wine to taupe to cream)	1 7/8 yd
Theme Fabric (with same basic color tones)	1 1/4 yd
Backing fabric: 42" x 55" (make sure fabric *is* 44")	1 3/4 yd
Batt: 45 x 60 (crib size batt)	
Thread: ecru for piecing and quilting	

Cutting Instructions

SuccesSecret
Prewash and <u>starch</u> fabrics. This lets fabric support doilies.

SuccesSecret
†If gradation runs perpendicular to selvage, treat like Four Fabric Alternative,: 2 medium & 2 dark fabric strips and 1 deep &1 light fabric strip.

<u>Gradated Fabric</u>†: Cut four 7 1/2" strips parallel to selvage, positioning strips to take advantage of color breaks and avoiding the palest color (on which doilies would be lost). Crosscut your deep and light strips into four 7 1/2" squares each; crosscut dark and medium strips into eight 7 1/2" squares each.

<u>Four Fabric Alternative</u>*: Cut one 7 1/2" strip from deep and light fabrics; crosscut four 7 1/2" squares each. Cut two 7 1/2" strips from dark and medium fabrics; crosscut eight 7 1/2" squares each.

<u>Theme Fabric</u>: Cut five 7 1/2" strips perpendicular to selvage. Crosscut into twenty-four 7 1/2" squares.

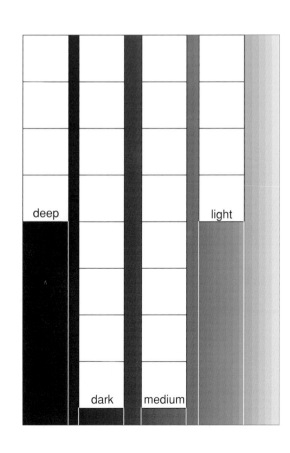

SYMPHONY
OF LACES

*Photograph
on page 24*

*Closeup
on page 25*

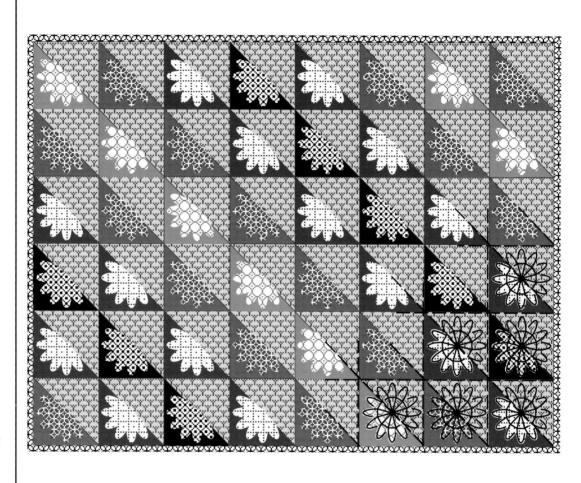

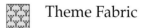

Finished Size:
39 3/4" x 53"
plus lace edging

Blocks: 48 total
6 5/8" finished
(7 1/8" w/seam
allowance) It
sounds like a
strange size, but
they're made
from easy to cut
7 1/2" squares!

Light:
8 blocks
(4 doilies)

Medium:
16 blocks
(8 doilies)

Dark:
16 blocks
(8 doilies)

Deep:
8 blocks
(4 doilies)

Light

Medium

Dark

Deep

Theme Fabric

- - Quilting

Lace Edging

Positioning Doilies

SuccesSecret
A white or silver pencil may show up better than regular lead on dark and deep colored squares.

SuccesSecret
Always place same doily on same colored fabric square -- that is, all deep squares with one doily style, all dark squares with another style doily, and so on.

Draw one diagonal line from corner to corner on *wrong* side of each 7 1/2" square of theme fabric.

Draw one diagonal line from corner to corner on *right* side of each 7 1/2" square of gradated fabric. Fold each in half on opposite diagonal and press lightly; open up.

With fabric right sides up, center doily over each gradated square. Put pin in doily center and through intersection of pressed and drawn diagonal lines. *For doilies with even number of scallops, rotate doily until drawn diagonal line goes through 'valleys'; pressed diagonal line may go through 'peaks' or 'valleys'. For doilies with odd number of scallops, rotate doily until 'peak' of one scallop is on pressed diagonal line and the opposite 'valley' is on other end of pressed line.*

As per general instructions, *lightly glue doily in place over drawn diagonal line and along doily edges.*

Make Half-Square Triangles

SuccesSecret
Using short stitch length prevents doilies from pulling out of seam.

SuccesSecret
Blocks should measure 7 1/8" square.

Right sides together, place 7 1/2" square of theme fabric over each gradated 7 1/2" square. Matching center intersections and diagonal lines, pin along diagonal lines.

With theme fabric on top, sew 1/4" along both sides of diagonal line. Press flat, then cut sections apart on diagonal line between stitches. Press seam towards theme fabric. Turn block over and press from front side.

The two blocks that started with even number of scallops on doily will look the same. The two blocks that started with odd number of scallops on doily will differ.

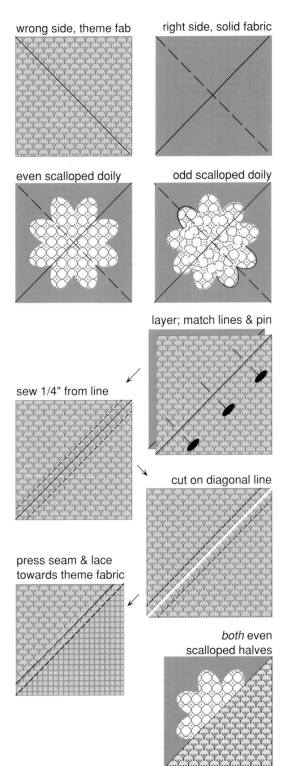

wrong side, theme fab

right side, solid fabric

even scalloped doily

odd scalloped doily

layer; match lines & pin

sew 1/4" from line

cut on diagonal line

press seam & lace towards theme fabric

both even scalloped halves

odd scalloped half

other odd scalloped half

Piece Quilt Top Together

SuccesSecret

Illustration is without doilies so gradation shows.

Arrange blocks as in diagram, gradated colors moving successively from one into the next and then back again: . . . . medium . . . dark . . . deep . . . dark . . . medium . . . light . . . medium . . . dark . . . deep . . . . The colors in each row are offset by one color step from previous row.

Sew blocks into rows; press seams in even rows one way and odd rows the other.

Butt seams and sew rows together. Press seams in one direction.

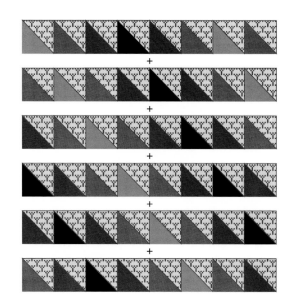

Finish Quilt

SuccesSecret

Use a cotton batt, but don't prewash it. When you wash finished quilt, batt will shrink slightly and quilting imperfections will sink into fabric!

Following instructions in Chapter 1, baste lace to edge of quilt top. Layer batt, quilt top (right side up) and backing (right side down). Stitch, leaving 15" opening; turn right side out and close opening. Stretch taut and baste layers together.

Using ecru thread, quilt all vertical, horizontal and diagonal seams "in the ditch".

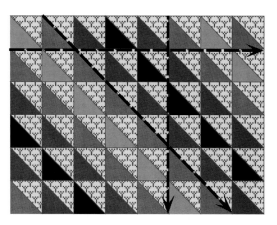

SuccesSecret

Use freezer paper to create doily 'shadows'. Since you quilt inside doily edge, cut paper a bit smaller than doily. Draw interior motifs on freezer paper as well; cut them out. 'Shadows' will look sort of like paper dolls. Iron waxed side to theme fabric.

Quilt each doily *and its shadow* in place by quilting around the edge. A doily's shadow is the image which would appear on the other half of the square (ie, on the theme fabric) if the doily weren't cut in half.

In addition, examine each doily style for key design elements *within* the doily and quilt these as well every time they appear. For example, small feathers appears throughout many pineapple doilies; quilt around them each time, or around the opening that surrounds the feather each time.

Find continous path between motifs. Quilt around each motif in both doily *and* its shadow in one pass.

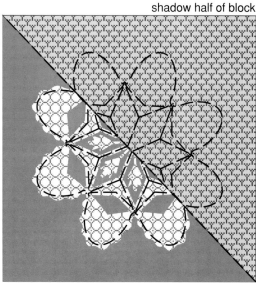

shadow half of block

doily half of block

35

Chapter 6
DRUNKARD'S DOILIES

Fabrics and Notions

SuccesSecret
If you can't find predyed doilies, buy white ones and use Dylon Cold Water Dye.

SuccesSecret
Vary navies & tans: plaids, vines, florals, some dark & some light.

6" Battenburg edged Doilies w/4 design scallops	
Tea-Dyed (Tan)	9
Navy Dyed	8
8 Different Tan prints	9" squares
8 Different Navy prints	9" squares
Topaz tone-on-tone *for inner border*	1/4 yd
Navy/Tan/Cream medium scale print *for border*	1/2 yd
Navy solid *for binding*	3/8 yd
Backing fabric: 35" x 35" (see page 39 for details)	1 1/8 yd

Batt: 35" square (see page 39 for details)
Thread: tan for piecing; tan and navy that match doilies for topstitching and slipstitching; tan and navy for quilting

Cutting Instructions

SuccesSecret
Prewash and <u>starch</u> fabrics before cutting. This gives fabric enough body to support doilies.

SuccesSecret
* Wait til quilt center is finished to crosscut topaz, border & solid navy fabrics.

<u>Tan Prints</u> and <u>Navy Prints</u>:
Cut 8" squares from each of eight tan and each of eight navy fabrics.

<u>Topaz tone-on-tone</u>: Cut four 1" wide strips; crosscut* into 30 1/4" lengths (quilt center measurement, including seam allowance, + 1 3/4").

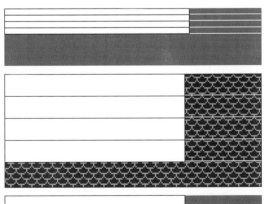

<u>Border fabric</u>: Cut four 3 1/4" wide strips; crosscut* into 29 1/2" lengths (quilt center measurement, including seam allowance, + 1").

<u>Navy solid</u>: Cut four 1 5/8" wide strips for hand-finished binding *or* 1 3/4" wide for stitched-in-ditch; crosscut* same length as border.

Drunkard's Doilies

Photograph on page 26

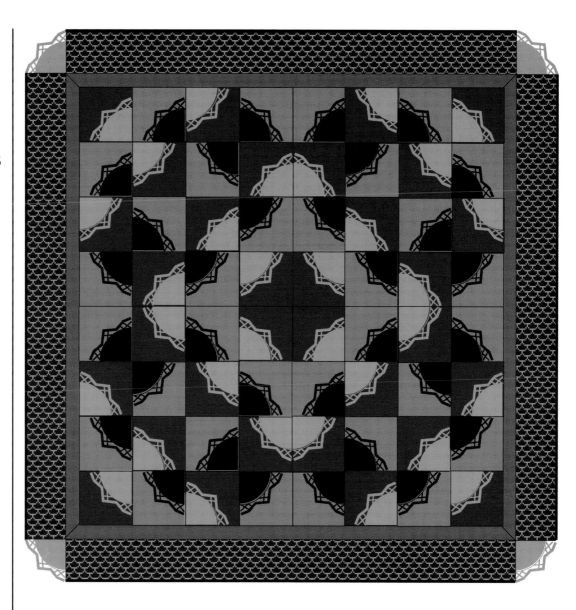

Finished Size:
35" x 35"

Blocks: 64 total (but made from just 16 squares!)
Finished Size: 3 1/2" (4" with seam allowance)

32 navy w/tan (4 of each fabric)

32 tan w/navy (4 of each fabric)

 Tan prints

 Navy prints

Topaz

Navy solid (binding)

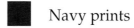 Navy/Tan/Cream print

Positioning Doilies

Draw vertical and horizontal center lines on right sides of 8" tan squares and 8" navy squares (4" in from edges).

SuccesSecret
Position doilies so fabric center's more heavily embroidered areas point towards corners of square.

With fabric right sides up, center doily over each square. Put pin in doily center and through intersection of lines. Rotate doily until lines go through secondary design scallop*. As per general instructions, *lightly glue doily in place over both lines and along doily edges.*

Zig-zag stitches contrasting for illustration only

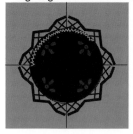

Make Quarter Square Blocks

Place thread in machine and bobbin to match doily. With fabric and doily right side up, narrowly zig-zag over stitches that already hold fabric center and lace edge together.

Fabric partially cut out and back of doily showing

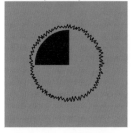

Turn doily over. Make slit through fabric. Insert scissors; trim out circle of fabric close to zig-zag stitches.

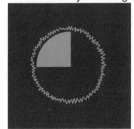

SuccesSecret
Since doilies are irregular, lace will come closer to outer edge on some blocks than on others. No one will notice when the quilt is done; if they do, tell them to get a life . . . !

Press flat from right side, making sure fabric is still 8" square. Cut sections apart on lines using rotary cutter and ruler's 4" line.

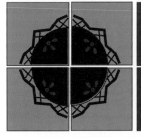

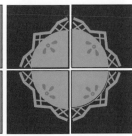

If you plan on quilting by hand, slipstitch edges of lace to fabric, using thread that matches lace.

Piece Quilt Center

Arrange blocks according to diagram on preceding page. Work a quarter at a time, using only one of each tan and navy fabric per quarter.

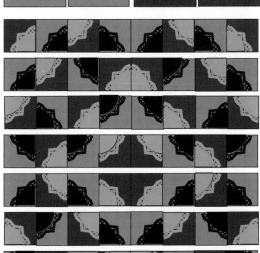

SuccesSecret
Arrange blocks on flannel board so you can step back and make sure you like where each individual fabric is placed.

Sew blocks together in rows using a short stitch length and tan thread. Press seams OPEN, including doily edges.

Sew rows together. Press seams open.

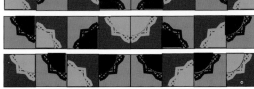

Add Borders

SuccesSecret

Quilt center should measure 28 1/2" across, <u>including</u> seam allowance. If it does, cut the four topaz strips to 30 1/4" lengths and border and binding strips to 29 1/2".

If quilt measures differently, add 1 3/4" to its measurement and cut the four 1" wide topaz strips to this length. Add 1" to the measurement and cut border and binding strips to this length.

Finish Quilt

SuccesSecret

Quilt across center <u>isn't</u> 35"? Adjust 29 1/2" & 35" up or down.

SuccesSecret

Quilt tan fabric with tan thread, navy fabric with navy. Quilt 1/4" from edge of lace and around fabric edges of blocks (page 26 photo).

Place 45° angle of ruler along edge of strip and cut off both corners so one side of strip is shorter than the other. On wrong side of strips, measure in 1/4" from each corner and mark intersections with dots.

With right sides together, pin topaz strips to top and bottom edges of quilt, pinning dots on strips' shorter sides 1/4" in from corner of quilt. Sew 1/4" seam, backstitching at dots at both ends of seam. Sew side topaz strips on in same manner, again backstitching into corners. Finger press seams away from topaz strips. Fold quilt on diagonal to corner. Sew miter, backstitching to outer dot at beginning of seam, forward to inner dot, then backstitching.

Quarter cut remaining tan doilies; sew to ends of two border strips, stretching lace if needed. Sew non-doilied border strips to sides of quilt, backstitching to dots on topaz inner border. Sew doilied borders to top and bottom. Press quilt center and border seams towards topaz strips.

Cut backing 35" wide across fabric; crosscut into one 29 1/2" strip and two 3 1/4" strips. Cut 3 1/4" strips to 29 1/2". Lay strips over rectangle's long sides, each end 2 3/4" from edge of rectangle. Sew, backstitching 1/4" from ends. Press seam to center.

Cut batt 35" square; cut 3" squares from corners. Baste layers together, matching raw edges. Turn open corners of backing under 1/4"; slipstitch over batt to doily seams. Quilt. Press binding strips in half, and turn end under 1/4". Sew to edge with 1/4" seam, backstitching at ends. Turn to back and slipstitch.

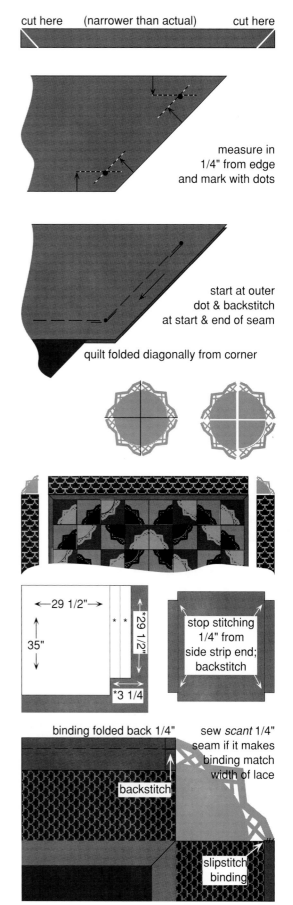

cut here   (narrower than actual)   cut here

measure in 1/4" from edge and mark with dots

start at outer dot & backstitch at start & end of seam

quilt folded diagonally from corner

stop stitching 1/4" from side strip end; backstitch

binding folded back 1/4"

sew *scant* 1/4" seam if it makes binding match width of lace

backstitch

slipstitch binding

Chapter 7
Do-Si-Doilies

Fabrics and Notions

SuccesSecret
Doily should show up easily on your lightest fabric. Also, consider having one of your fabrics be a plaid or stripe.

4" Ecru Doilies with Eight (8) Scallops	9
Small Brass Heart Charm	1
Salmon (medium light)	1/4 yd
Focus Floral (medium) *includes border*	1/2 yd
Rust (medium-dark)	1/4 yd
Navy (dark) *includes binding*	3/8 yd
Backing fabric: 22 - 24" square	3/4 yd

Batt: 22 - 24" square
Thread: neutral for piecing; ecru (blends with doilies) and light blue (blends with focus floral and navy fabrics) for quilting.

Cutting Instructions

SuccesSecret
Prewash and <u>starch</u> fabrics before cutting. This gives fabric enough body to support doilies.

<u>Salmon (medium light):</u>
Cut one strip 5 1/4" wide; crosscut into four 5 1/4" squares. Cut one 5" square from remainder of strip.

<u>Focus Floral (medium):</u>
Cut one strip 5 1/4" wide; crosscut into four 5 1/4" squares. Cut two 2 1/2" strips; crosscut into four 16 1/2" segments (may wait until ready to add borders to do crosscut).

<u>Rust (medium-dark):</u>
Cut one strip 5 1/4" wide; crosscut into four 5 1/4" squares.

<u>Navy (dark):</u>
Cut one strip 5 1/4" wide; crosscut into four 5 1/4" squares. Cut two strips 1 5/8" wide if hand-finishing binding *or* cut two strips 1 3/4" wide if finishing binding by machine.

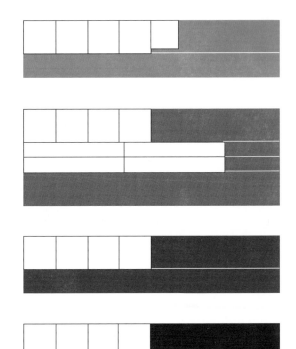

Do - Si - Doilies

Photograph on page 27

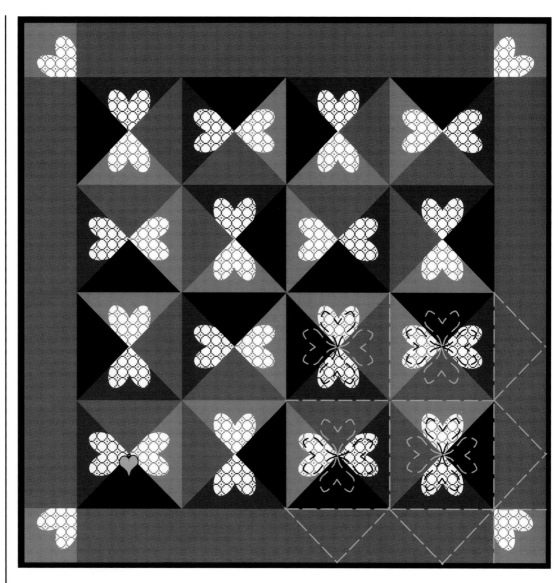

Finished Size:
20 1/2" x 20 1/2"

Blocks: 16 total
(8 of each fabric rotation)
Finished Size: 4"
(4 1/2" w/seam allowance)

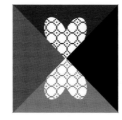

Corner Blocks: 4
Finished Size: 2"
(2 1/2" w/seam allowance)

Salmon (medium-light)

Focus Floral (medium)

Rust (medium-dark)

Navy (dark)

 Ecru Quilting Thread

 Light Blue Quilting Thread

Brass Heart Charm

Positioning Doilies

SuccesSecret
Draw lines while on the phone or while watching your favorite TV show.

Draw two diagonal lines from corner to corner on *wrong* side of *all* 5 1/4" squares (all four colors).

Draw two diagonal lines from corner to corner on *right* side of all salmon (medium-light) and rust (medium-dark) 5 1/4" squares.

With fabric right sides up, center doily over each salmon (medium-light) and rust (medium-dark) 5 1/4" squares. Put pin in doily center and through intersection of diagonal lines. Rotate doily until diagonal lines go through 'valleys'. As per general instructions, *lightly* glue doily in place over both diagonal lines and along doily edges.

Make Half-Square Triangles

SuccesSecret
Make sure doilies are layered in-between squares.

SuccesSecret
Be sure to use a short stitch length.

Right sides together, place 5 1/4" square of focus floral (medium) over each salmon (medium-light) 5 1/4" square; and 5 1/4" navy (dark) square over each rust (medium-dark) 5 1/4" square. Matching center intersections and diagonal lines; pin along one of the diagonal lines.

With non-doilied square on top, sew 1/4" along both sides of diagonal line; ignore 2nd diagonal line for the moment. Press flat, then cut sections apart on diagonal line between stitches. Press seams OPEN, with doily edges pressed towards salmon (medium-light) and rust (medium-dark) fabrics.

Make Quarter-Square Triangles

Right sides together and with doilies laying in opposing directions, layer salmon & focus floral square over navy & rust square. Match centers and diagonal lines; pin. Sew 1/4" along both sides of diagonal line; seams should remain open at center.

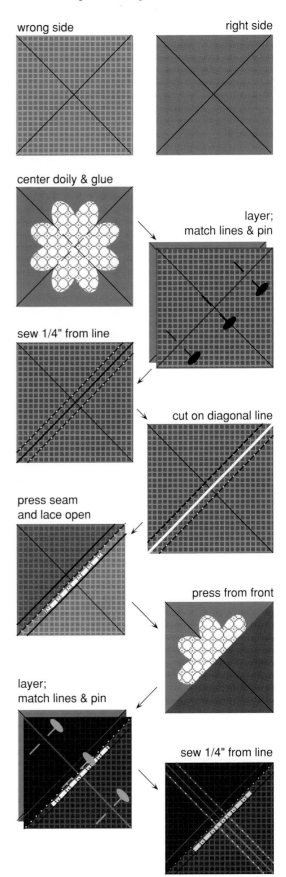

Shown using medium-light & medium fabrics

wrong side

right side

center doily & glue

layer; match lines & pin

sew 1/4" from line

cut on diagonal line

press seam and lace open

press from front

layer; match lines & pin

sew 1/4" from line

SuccesSecret
Blocks should measure 4 1/2" square.

Press flat; cut apart on diagonal line between stitches. Press seams OPEN, with doily edges pressed towards salmon (medium-light) and rust (medium-dark) fabrics.

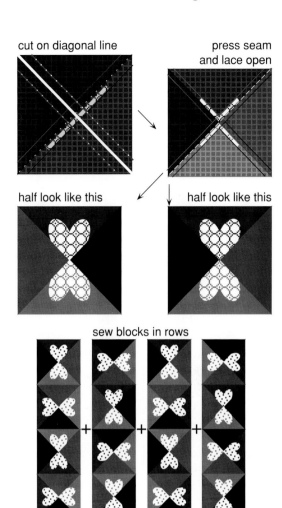

cut on diagonal line

press seam and lace open

half look like this

half look like this

Piece Quilt Top Together

SuccesSecret
Butt seams when sewing rows together.

Arrange blocks as in diagram, navy and rust fabrics (dark and medium-dark) at outer edges of quilt, navy pin-wheel at quilt center and doilies alternating directions between blocks. Sew blocks into rows; press seams away from doilies. Sew rows together. Press seams in one direction.

sew blocks in rows

Add Borders

Draw vertical and horizontal center lines on right sides of 5" salmon (medium-light) square (2 1/2" in from edges). Center and lightly glue remaining doily in place with 'valleys' over lines. Cut into quarters.

With right sides together, sew border strips to top and bottom edges of quilt; press seams towards border. Sew corner squares to ends of remaining border strips (corners of hearts pointing in); press seams towards border. Butting seams at corners, sew borders to quilt's sides; press seams towards border.

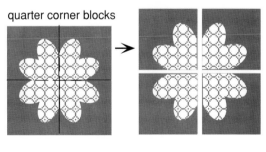

quarter corner blocks

Finish Quilt

SuccesSecret
Except when crossing at block's center, avoid quilting in diagonal seams.

SuccesSecret
Add a single brass heart to one block.

Baste quilt layers together. Quilt all horizontal and vertical seams "in the ditch" with light blue thread. Quilt through edges of doilies with ecru thread; quilt "shadow" hearts in focus floral and navy triangles.

Extend diagonal lines in quilt into border, ending lines 1/4" in from edge. Quilt with light blue thread. Fold binding in half and sew on 1/4" from edge. Turn to back and finish.

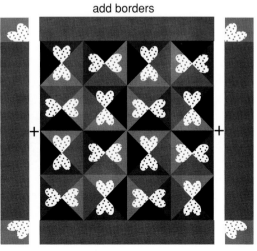

add borders

Chapter 8
LACE AND MARMALADE

Fabrics and Notions

SuccesSecret
Accented Black means black with red dots or black with purple stars. Can't find your accent color? Buy a black with white fabric and overdye with Dylon Cold Water Dye.

6" White Doilies with Six (6) Scallops each	8
Focus Fabric: Multicolored on Black with White	5/8 yd
Four assorted Bright tone-on-tone fabrics: Red, Purple, Gold and Green	1/2 yd each
Four assorted Accented Black* fabrics with one color each: Red, Purple, Gold and Green	1/2 yd each
Solid Black *for binding*	5/8 yd
Backing fabric: 44" x 49" (make sure fabric *is* 44-45")	1 1/2 yd
Batt: 49" x 49"	
Thread: black for piecing; black and white for quilting	

Optional: 8 sheets Triangle Paper™, 2 1/2" finished size, Yield: 24 sq/sheet (SPPS, Inc. 4410 N. Rancho Dr. #165, Las Vegas, NV 89130, 702-658-7988)

Cutting Instructions

SuccesSecret
Prewash all fabrics separately to check for color run. Wash several times to get excess dye out. If they still run, don't use that fabric unless you want your white doilies tinted! Once you know your colors are stable, starch fabrics. This keeps all the bias seams firmly in place!

Focus Fabric: Cut two 8 3/8" wide strips; crosscut into eight 8 3/8" squares.

4 Bright Fabrics: Cut two 11" wide strips parallel to selvage; crosscut into two 11" x 14 1/2" rectangles. Cut one 8 3/8" wide strip at right angles to selvage across fabric width; crosscut into two 8 3/8" squares.

Four Accented Black Fabrics: Cut two 11" wide strips parallel to selvage; cut each into 11" x 14 1/2" rectangles. Cut 3" wide strip; crosscut to four 3" squares per fabric.

Black: *not shown* Cut five strips 3 1/8" wide if hand-finished binding *or* 3 1/4" wide if stitching-in-ditch.

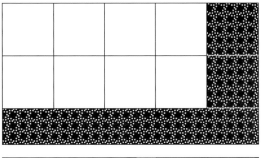

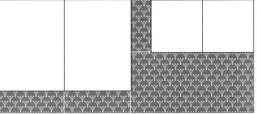

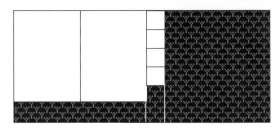

LACE AND MARMALADE

Photograph on page 28

Finished Size:
45" x 45"

Blocks: 16 total
4 w/each Bright
large triangle
10" finished
(10 1/2" with
seam allowance)

**Small Triangles
and Squares:**
2 1/2" finished
(3" with seam
allowance)

Large Triangles
7 1/2" finished
(8" with seam
allowance)

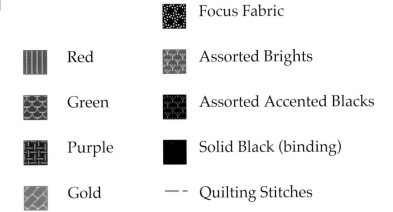

Focus Fabric

Red

Assorted Brights

Green

Assorted Accented Blacks

Purple

Solid Black (binding)

Gold

-- Quilting Stitches

Positioning Doilies

SuccesSecret
A white or silver pencil may show up better than regular lead on dark colored squares.

Draw one diagonal line from corner to corner on *wrong* side of each 8 3/8" square of Focus Fabric.

Draw one diagonal line from corner to corner on *right* side of each 8 3/8" square of Bright fabric. Fold each in half on opposite diagonal and press lightly; open up.

With fabric right sides up, center doily over each Bright square. Put pin in doily center and through intersection of pressed and drawn diagonal lines. Rotate doily until drawn diagonal line goes through 'valleys'; pressed diagonal line goes through 'peaks'. As per general instructions, *lightly* glue doily in place over drawn diagonal line and along doily edges.

Make Large Half-Square Triangles

SuccesSecret
Using short stitch length prevents doilies from pulling out of seam.

Right sides together, place 8 3/8" square of Focus Fabric over each Bright 8 3/8" square. Matching center intersections and diagonal lines, pin along diagonal lines.

With Focus Fabric on top, sew 1/4" along both sides of diagonal line. Press flat, then cut sections apart on diagonal line between stitches. Press seam towards Focus Fabric. Turn block over and press from front side. Blocks should measure 8" square.

Make Small Half-Square Triangles

SuccesSecret
Triangle Paper™, listed on page 44, does grids & lines for you!

On wrong side of each 11" x 14 1/2" Bright rectangle, draw grid 3 squares wide by 4 squares tall, each square being 3 3/8" big. Draw diagonal lines through grids as illustrated. Pair up with Accented Black fabrics, avoiding color matches, right sides together and sew 1/4" on either side of diagonal lines. Cut into triangles; press open as with large triangles.

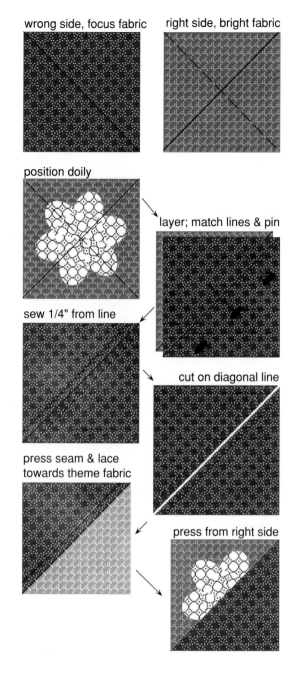

wrong side, focus fabric   right side, bright fabric

position doily

layer; match lines & pin

sew 1/4" from line

cut on diagonal line

press seam & lace towards theme fabric

press from right side

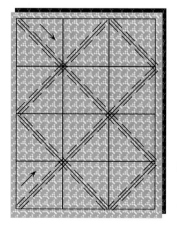

24 squares 3" big
(2 1/2" finished)
from each set =
192 total squares

Make Blocks

SuccesSecret

Arrange units so Bright color in large triangle does not appear in that block's small Bright triangles. Have Accented Black corner square match color of large Bright triangle.

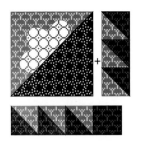
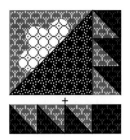
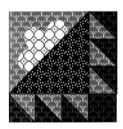

Arrange small half-square triangles and squares around large half-square triangles, as shown. Mix up colors until a pleasing arrangement is formed. Sew small half-square triangles and squares into units; press seams away from center triangle set on each side.

Sew unit without square to Focus Fabric side of large half-square triangle; press seam towards Focus Fabric. Sew unit with square to remaining side of large half-square triangle, butting seams at corner; press seam away from Focus Fabric.

Sew Quilt Top

SuccesSecret

There is no right or wrong way to arrange the small colored triangles; just have fun!

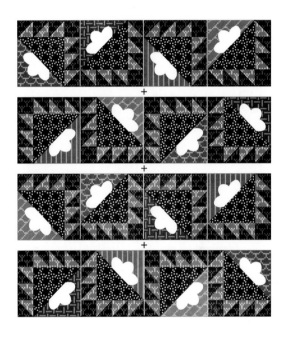

Arrange blocks with color placement of large Bright triangles as shown in diagram and in photo on page 28. Sew together in rows; press seams towards large triangles. Butt seams and sew rows together; press one way. Arrange half-square triangle units for border, mixing colors and twisting and turning; sew together. Sew to sides of quilt center, then top and bottom.

Finish Quilt

SuccesSecret

* Cut quilt back in two unequal parts lengthwise. Chain leftover 3" half-square triangle units to equal 49". Insert to widen backing.

SuccesSecret

Bind with solid black, stitching 1/2" from edge.

Baste quilt back* (right side down), batt, and top (right side up) together.

Using black thread, quilt "in ditch": vertical and horizontal seams around blocks; seams connecting small units to large triangles; diagonal seams between large triangles.

Using white thread, quilt each doily *and its shadow* in place by quilting around doily edge and major motifs. A doily's shadow is the image which would appear on the other half of the square (ie, on the Focus Fabric) if the doily weren't cut in half. (*see page 35 for details on shadow quilting*).

SOURCES OF SPECIALTY ITEMS

Doilies

I used a wide variety of doilies for the projects in this book. If you are unable to find appropriate doilies at your local quilting, fabric or craft store, contact:

THROUGH THE SCREEN DOOR
PO Box 505 - DM2
Columbia, MO 65205-0505
Orders (USA): 1-800-889-6213
Phone: 573-256-7078
Website: www.sharonrexroad.com

We usually stock doilies appropriate for the following projects:
In Love with Lace • Drunkard's Doilies • Do-Si-Doilies • I ♥ My Secret Sister

OTHER PUBLICATIONS BY SHARON REXROAD

Books

A Christmas of Angels
A Romance with Blue & White
Let's Bee Quiltin'

Doily Magic Patterns

Autumn Lace
Butterfly Kisses
Fans of the Happy Couple
Lace-Spangled Banner
Wreath of Gold

Foundation Piecing

Tea and Chintz pattern series
Serendipidity Sampler pattern series

Available at Quilt Shops or directly from:

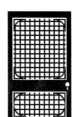

THROUGH THE SCREEN DOOR
PO Box 505 - DM2
Columbia, MO 65205-0505
Orders (USA): 1-800-889-6213
Phone: 573-256-7078
Website: www.sharonrexroad.com

Call for a FREE Catalog of **THROUGH THE SCREEN DOOR**'s products.